Herbert Puchta   Günter Gerngross   Peter Lewis-Jones

Super Minds

Workbook 1 with Online Resources

CAMBRIDGE
UNIVERSITY PRESS

CAMBRIDGE
UNIVERSITY PRESS

University Printing House, Cambridge CB2 8BS, United Kingdom

One Liberty Plaza, 20th Floor, New York, NY 10006, USA

477 Williamstown Road, Port Melbourne, VIC 3207, Australia

4843/24, 2nd Floor, Ansari Road, Daryaganj, Delhi – 110002, India

79 Anson Road, #06–04/06, Singapore 079906

Cambridge University Press is part of the University of Cambridge.

It furthers the University's mission by disseminating knowledge in the pursuit of education, learning and research at the highest international levels of excellence.

www.cambridge.org
Information on this title: www.cambridge.org/9781107482951

First published 2014
20 19 18

Printed in Dubai by Oriental Press

A catalogue record for this publication is available from the British Library

ISBN 978-1-107-48295-1 Workbook 1 with Online Resources
ISBN 978-0-521-14855-9 Student's Book with DVD-ROM 1
ISBN 978-0-521-22061-3 Teacher's Book 1
ISBN 978-1-107-66604-7 Teacher's Resource Book 1
ISBN 178-0-521-22136-8 Class Audio CDs 1
ISBN 978-0-521-22026-2 Flashcards 1
ISBN 978-1-107-44123-1 Presentation Plus DVD-ROM 1
ISBN 978-1-107-42962-8 Tests CD-ROM 1–2
ISBN 978-1-107-42782-2 Posters Starter–2

Contents

Friends

1 **Match the sentences with the pictures. Colour the circles.**

◯ I'm Whisper. ◯ I'm Flash. ◯ I'm Thunder. ◯ I'm Misty.

1 **Match the numbers with the words.**

9 5 4

8 7 3

6 10

2 1

seven

three

ten

eight

nine

one

four

five

two

six

2 **Write the numbers.**

three _3_

one _____

six _____

two _____

seven _____

nine _____

eight _____

four _____

ten _____

five _____

1 Write the missing letters.

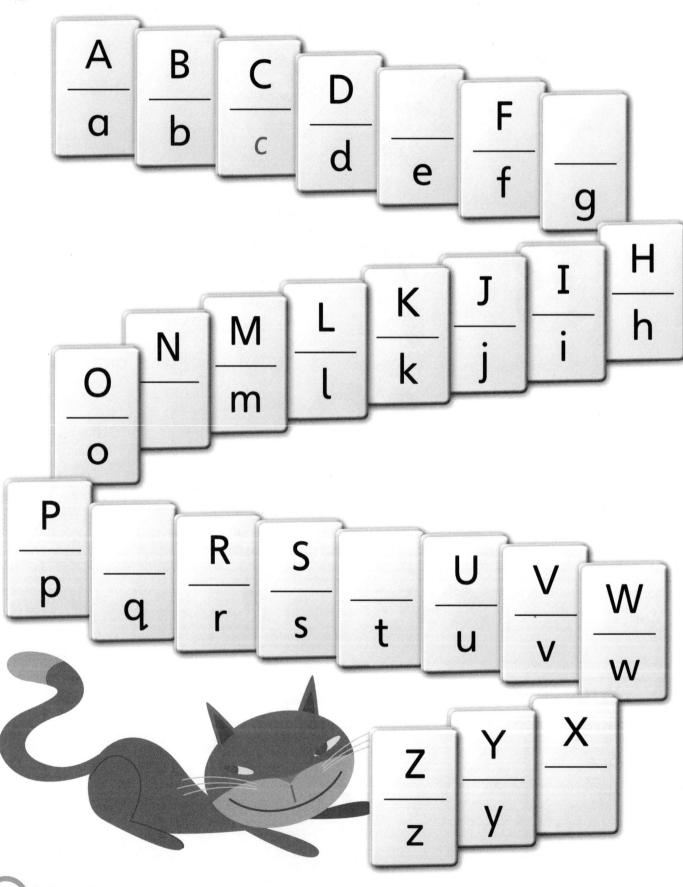

A / a
B / b
C / c
D / d
E / e
F / f
G / g
H / h
I / i
J / j
K / k
L / l
M / m
N / n
O / o
P / p
Q / q
R / r
S / s
T / t
U / u
V / v
W / w
X / x
Y / y
Z / z

1 Colour the words.

yellow   purple

red   green

orange   blue

2 Write and draw.

Hi, I'm _____ .
My hat is _____ . Look!

1 **CD 1 11** Listen and tick (✓) the box.

1

2

3

2 Match the Super Friends with the powers.

1

a

2

b

3

c

4

d

My Super Mind

1   **Draw and write examples of what you know.**

1

I'm six.

2

3

4

1 At school

1 **Match the words with the pictures.**

1 desk   **2** bag   **3** pencil

4 notebook   **6** book

5 rubber   **7** pen

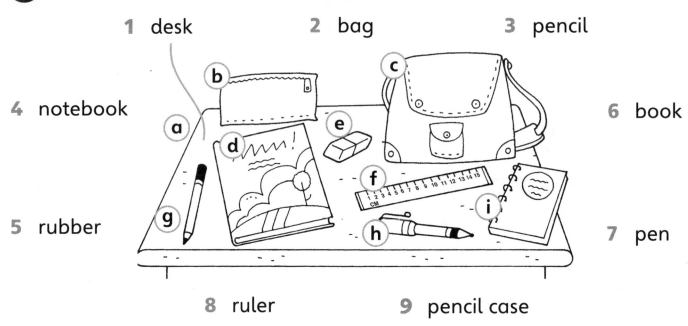

8 ruler   **9** pencil case

2 **Look and colour.**

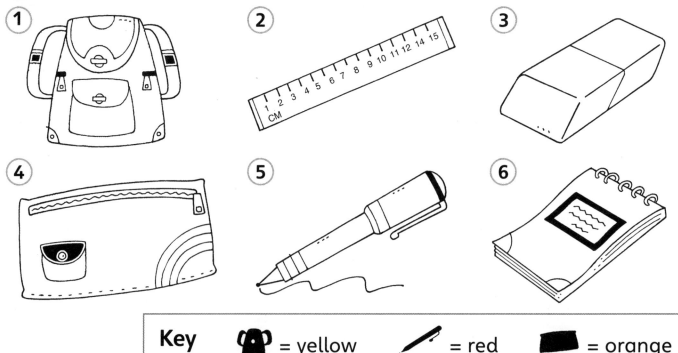

Key

= yellow   = red   = orange

= purple   = blue   = green

1 CD1 16 Listen and write the words.

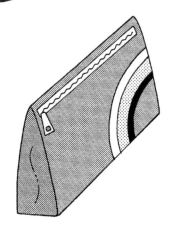 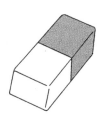 

1 _pencil_   2 _____

3 _____   4 _____

2 Read and tick (✓) the box.

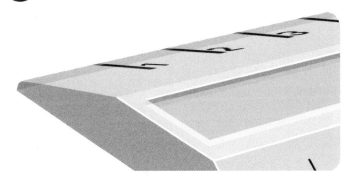 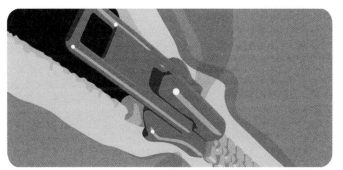

1 What's this? Is it a ruler?
  ✓ Yes, it is. ☐ No, it isn't.

2 What's this? Is it a pencil case?
  ☐ Yes, it is. ☐ No, it isn't.

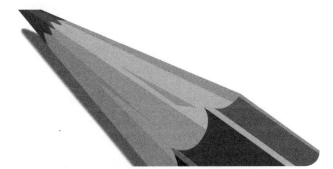 

3 What's this? Is it a rubber?
  ☐ Yes, it is. ☐ No, it isn't.

4 What's this? Is it a pencil?
  ☐ Yes, it is. ☐ No, it isn't.

Follow the lines and make sentences.

It's my …   It isn't my …

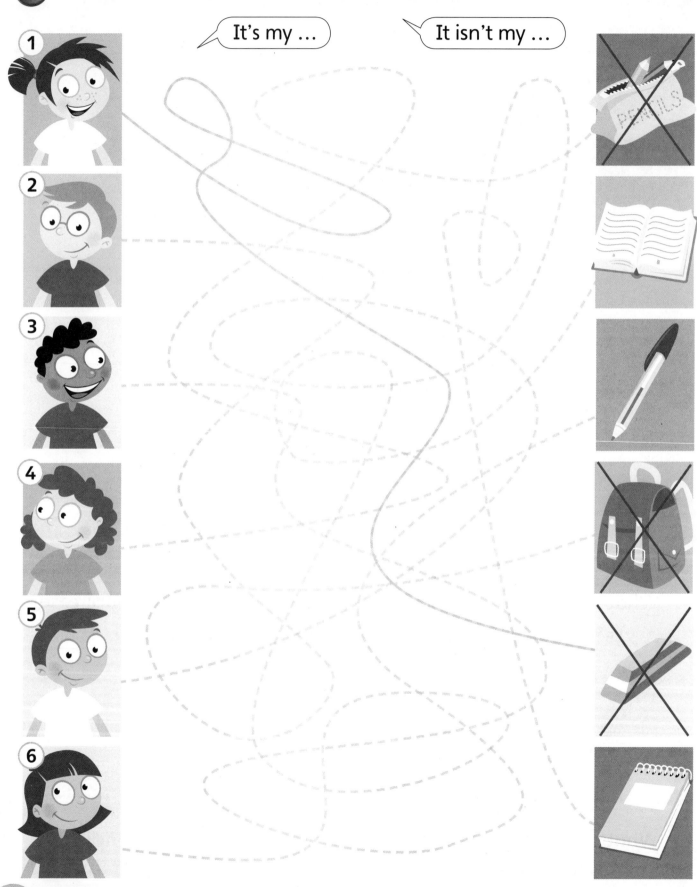

1 Read and write the words.

1 Pass me a 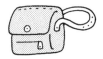 _pencil_ .

2 Close your .

3 Open your  .

4 Pass me a .

5 Sit at your .

2 Read and match. Write numbers.

1 Close your pencil case. **a** ☐

2 Pass me a ruler, please. **b** ☐

3 Open your book. **c** 1

4 Pass me a notebook, please. **d** ☐

5 Close your book. **e** ☐

1 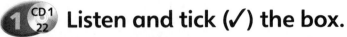 **Listen and tick (✓) the box.**

1    **2**    **3**

2 **Look at the story. Find Flash and write the number.**

a    **b**    **c**    **d**

Picture _1_   Picture _____   Picture _____   Picture _____

3 **Think!** **Write the numbers.**

☐ Thank you.   1 I'm sorry.   ☐ It's OK.

Watch out!

1

2

Here you are!

3

1 Values Look and circle.

2 CD1 24 **Write and match. Listen and say.**

1 A c a t   a ☐

2 A f__t r__t   b ☐ 1

3 A bl__ck b__g   c ☐

4 A bl__ck h__t   d ☐

1   **Look and read. Put a tick (✓) or a cross (✗) in the box.**

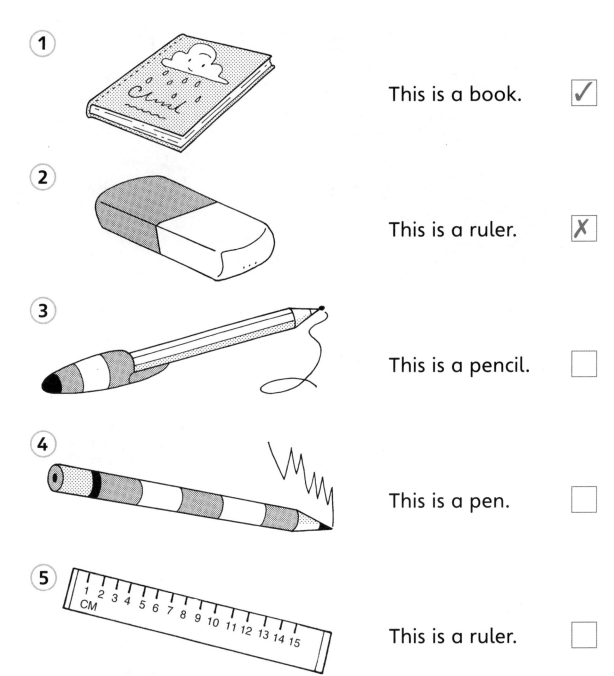

1   This is a book. ✓

2   This is a ruler. ✗

3   This is a pencil. ☐

4   This is a pen. ☐

5   This is a ruler. ☐

6   This is a notebook. ☐

1 CD1 26 **Listen and number.**

1 Complete the colour chart.

> purple ~~red~~ blue green yellow orange

Primary colours	Secondary colours
red	

2 Read, write and colour.

1 blue + yellow = _green_

2 yellow + red = _____

3 red + blue = _____

1 Colour the picture.

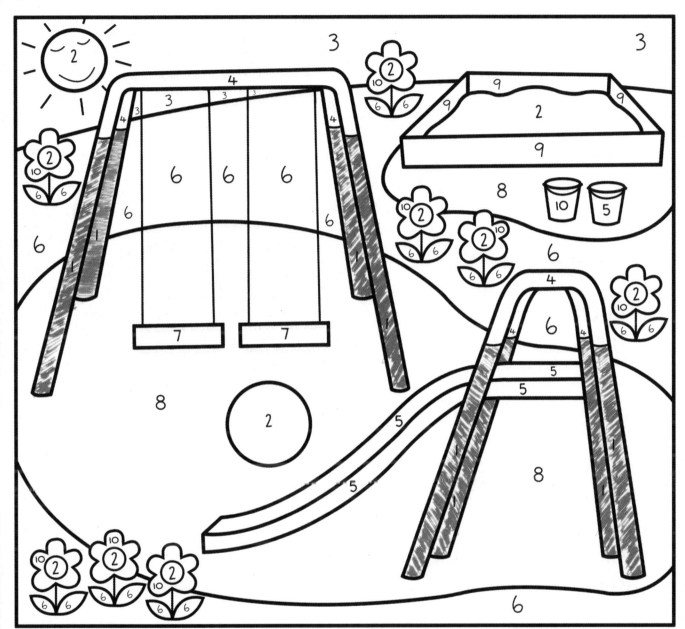

Key

1 = grey	5 = red	9 = orange
2 = yellow	6 = green	10 = pink
3 = blue	7 = black	
4 = purple	8 = white	

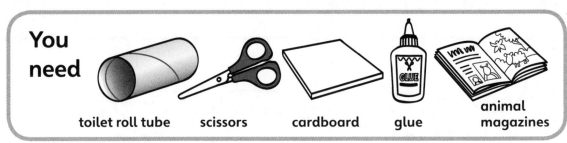

Crafts

1 **Make a pencil holder.**

You need

toilet roll tube   scissors   cardboard   glue   animal magazines

1

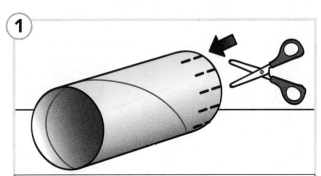

Cut flaps at the bottom of the toilet roll tube.

2

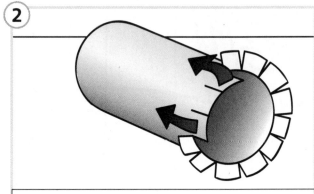

Fold the flaps out.

3

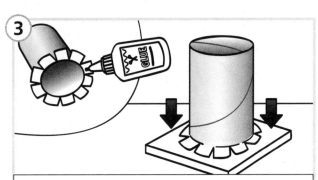

Glue the flaps on the piece of cardboard.

4

Cut out pictures of animals from magazines.

5

Glue the pictures on the tube.

6

Now you have a pencil holder.

My Super Mind

1 Draw and write examples of what you know.

1

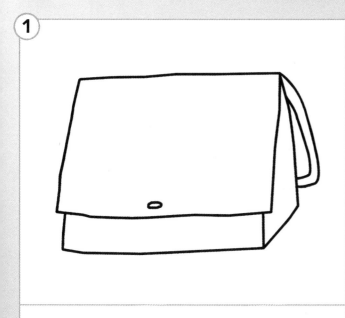

Is it your bag?

2

3

4

Let's play!

1 CD 1 30 **Listen and number.**

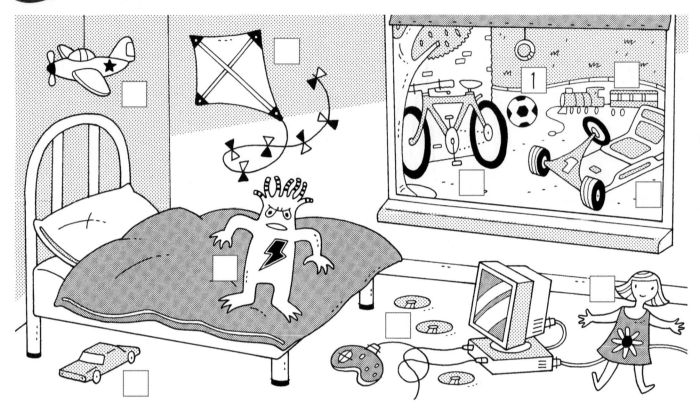

2 **Join the dots. What is it?** _____

1 Follow the lines. Write the words.

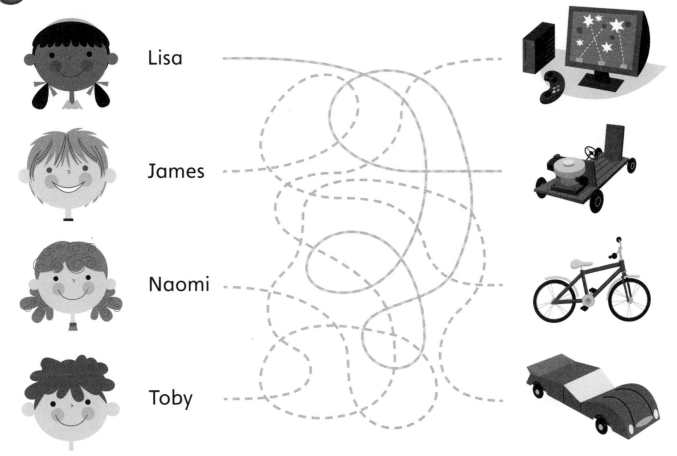

Lisa

James

Naomi

Toby

1 Her name's Lisa. Her favourite toy is her _go-kart_ .

2 His name's James. His favourite toy is his _____ .

3 Her name's Naomi. Her favourite toy is her _____ .

4 His name's Toby. His favourite toy is his _____ .

2 Read and match. Write numbers.

1 What's her name? _____ She's seven.

2 How old is Mary? _____ Her favourite toy is her doll.

3 What's her favourite toy? __1__ Mary.

4 What's his name? _____ Henry.

5 How old is Henry? _____ His favourite toy is his bike.

6 What's his favourite toy? _____ He's six.

1 Look at the song. Circle the picture.

Her favourite toy is ...

His favourite number is ...

2 Write a new verse about you. Draw a picture.

Hey, _____ ! What's _____
_____ colour?

My favourite _____
   isn't _____ .

It isn't _____ or _____ .

My favourite _____ ,

My favourite colour's _____ .

That's great!

1 CD1 37 **Listen and tick (✓) the box.**

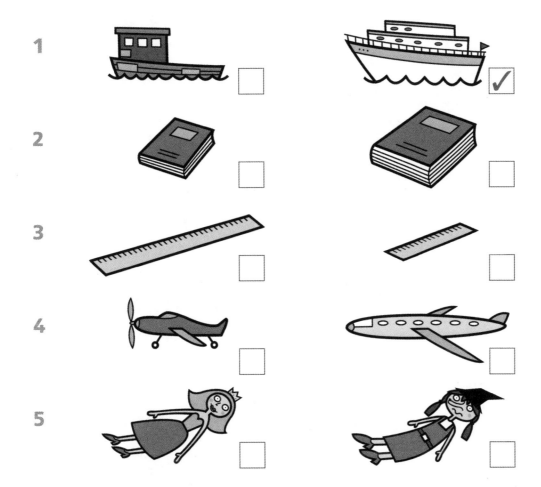

1

2

3

4

5

2 **Write the words in order.**

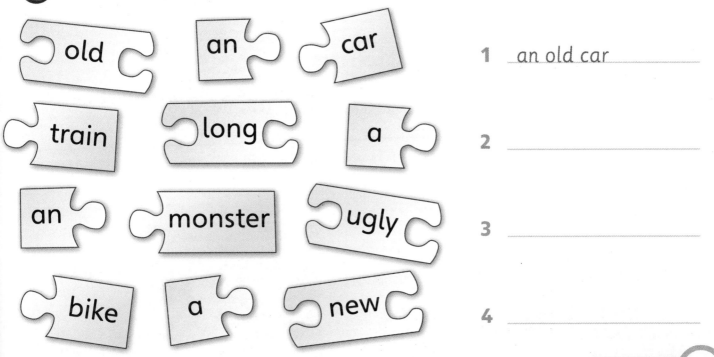

1 _an old car_

2 _____

3 _____

4 _____

1 CD1 39 Listen and tick (✓) the box.

1

2

3

2 Think! Put the story in order.

a

Picture _____

e

Picture _____

b

Picture _____

f

Picture _____

c

Picture _____

g

Picture _____

d

Picture _1_

h

Picture _____

1 (Values) **Look and circle.**

1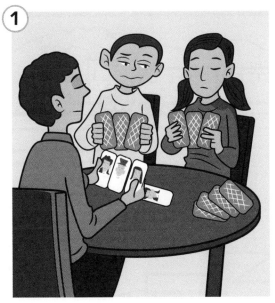

2

2 CD1 41 **Write _e_ or _a_. Listen and say.**

1 c a t

2  p__n

3  p__ncil

4  b__g

5  d__sk

6  t__n

7  bl__ck

8  Fl__sh

1 Read, number and colour.

1 an ugly yellow doll

2 a long blue train

3 a small green monster

4 a new black bike

5 a short red train

6 an old purple bike

7 a big black monster

8 a beautiful pink doll

1 **Listen and number.**

1

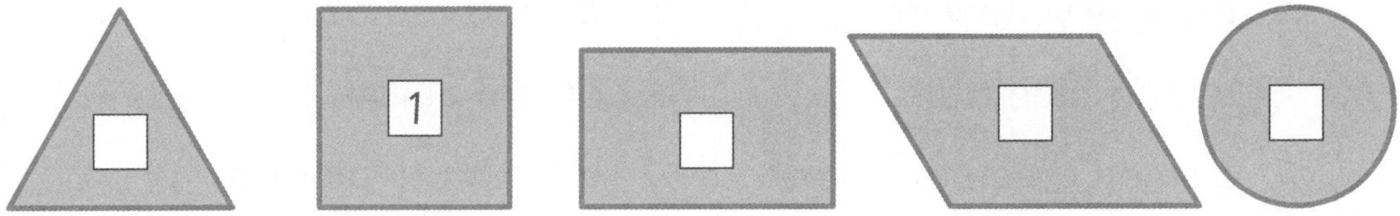

2 **Read and draw.**

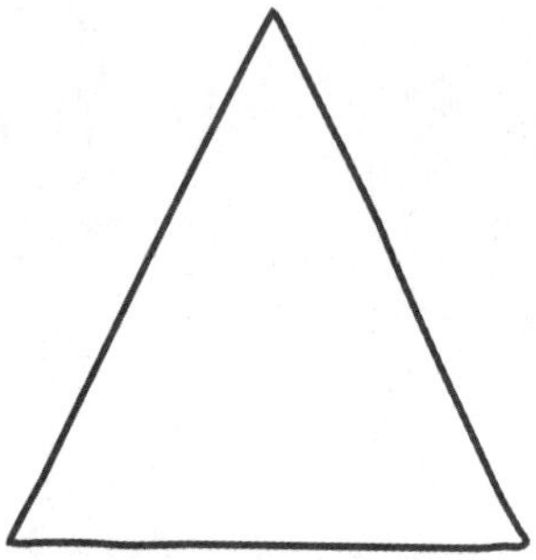

1 a red triangle

2 a green square

3 a blue circle

4 a pink parallelogram

5 a yellow rectangle

1 **Think!** Tick (✓) the picture you can make with the pieces of the tangram.

(a)

(b)

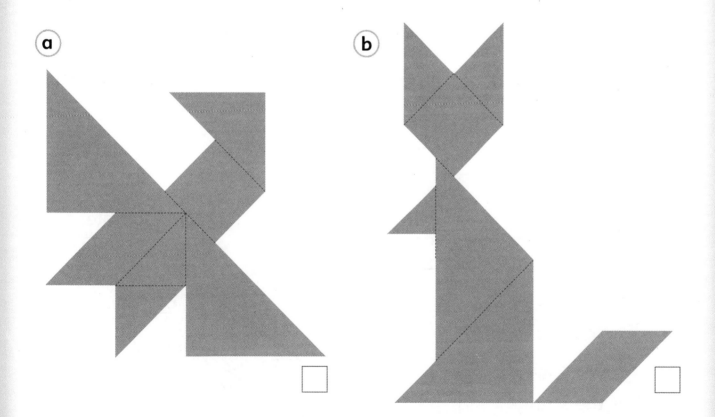

1 **Make a paper kite.**

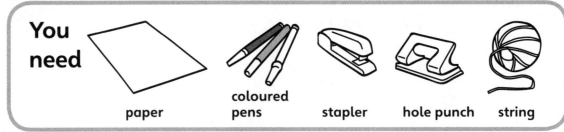

You need — paper · coloured pens · stapler · hole punch · string

1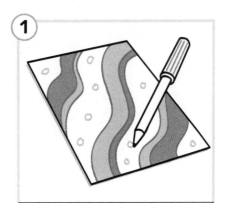

Colour the paper.

2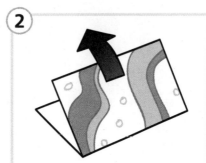

Fold the paper in half.

3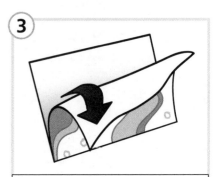

Bend one side of the paper.

4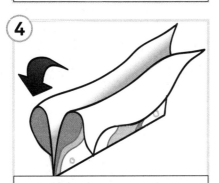

Bend the other side.

5

Staple the corners.

6

Make a hole.

7

Put the string through the hole and tie a knot.

8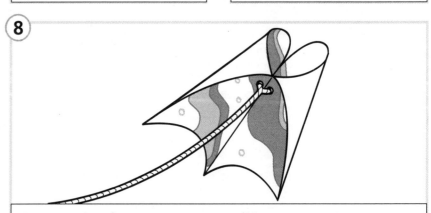

Now you have a paper kite.

My Super Mind

1 **Draw and write examples of what you know.**

1

My favourite toy's a plane.

2

3

4

3 Pet show

1 Look and write the words.

spider lizard ~~elephant~~
duck rat dog cat frog

1

| ¹e | ²l | e | p | h | a | n | t |

4

3

5 6   7

8

2 Write and draw.

My favourite animal is a _____ . Look!

34 Animals

1 Look and tick (✓) the box.

1	The elephant is under the car.	✓ Yes	☐ No
2	The cat is on the car.	☐ Yes	☐ No
3	The frog is in the car.	☐ Yes	☐ No
4	The spider is on the car.	☐ Yes	☐ No
5	The duck is in the car.	☐ Yes	☐ No

2 Read and draw.

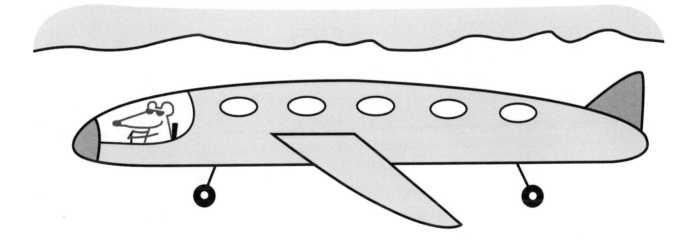

1 Draw a rat in the plane. **3** Draw a lizard on the plane.

2 Draw a dog under the plane. **4** Draw a spider under the plane.

1 Match the pictures with the words.

dogs

an elephant

elephants

rats

a frog

a cat

a dog

frogs

cats

a rat

1 CD1 56 **Listen and draw a happy mouth or a sad mouth.**

	🐕	🐈	🕷	🐘
Fiona	☺	☺	☺	☺
Andrew	☺	☺	☺	☺

2 **Match the pictures with the sentences. Colour the circles.**

🔘 I like ducks.

◯ I don't like frogs.

◯ I like frogs.

◯ I like lizards.

◯ I don't like lizards.

◯ I don't like ducks.

1 CD 1 58 **Listen and tick (✓) the box.**

1

2

3

2 **Look at the story. Find the pictures and write the number.**

a

b

c

d

Picture _4_   Picture _____   Picture _____   Picture _____

3 Think! **Match the pictures with the sentences.**

a

b

1 It's beautiful.

2 They're beautiful.

3 Wow! A monster.

4 A go-kart.

5 Wow! Two ugly monsters.

6 She's great.

c

e

f

d

1 (Values) Look and circle.

1

2

2 CD1 60 Read, draw and colour. Listen and say.

1 a big pan

2 six pens

3 a pink desk

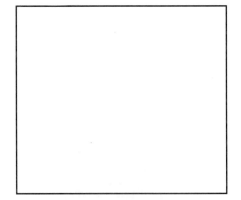

4 a black rat

5 a red cat

6 ten bags

1 Listen and draw lines.

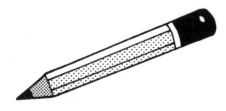

1 **Look and write the numbers.**

Come to the zoo. See the animals.

Two elephants, _____ ducks, _____ frogs, _____ lizards and _____ spider.

1 Think! **Colour the picture. Hide the lizard.**

2 Find the differences.

Picture one. Two snakes.
Picture two. Three snakes.

1

2

1 **Find the animals and write the words.**

1 The ___tiger___
is in the grass.

2 The _____
is in the tree.

3 The _____
is on the log.

4 The _____
is on the flower.

2 **Match the pictures with the words.**

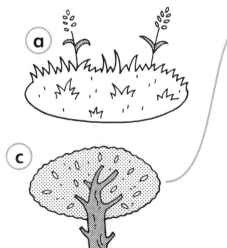

a

c

1 tree

2 log

3 leaf

4 flower

5 grass

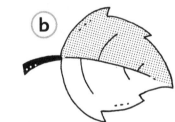

b

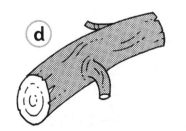

d

e

1 **Make an animal mask.**

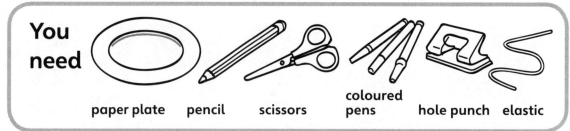

You need

paper plate   pencil   scissors   coloured pens   hole punch   elastic

1

Put the paper plate on your face. Your teacher marks where your eyes are.

2

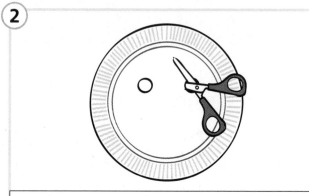

Your teacher cuts out the eyes.

3

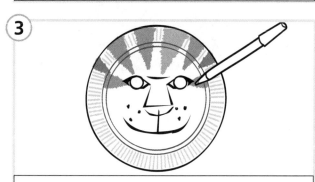

Colour the mask and draw a nose and a mouth.

4

Your teacher makes two holes at the sides.

5

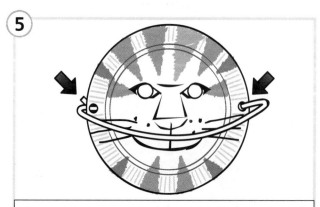

Tie elastic to the two sides.

6

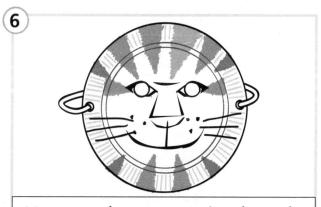

Now you have an animal mask.

My Super Mind

1 Draw and write examples of what you know.

1

The frog is under the flower.

2

3

4

1 **Write the numbers.**

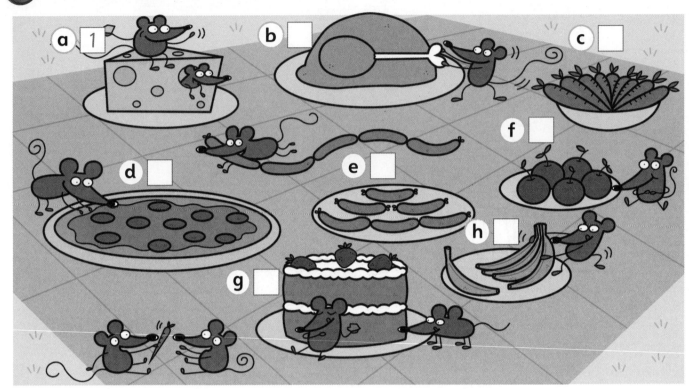

Key

1 = cheese	2 = pizza	3 = chicken	4 = sausages
5 = apples	6 = cake	7 = carrots	8 = bananas

2 **Think!** **Find the words.**

peasteakitecarrotrainsausagelephantpizzapple

1 CD2 05 Listen and write the letters *A–F* on the rats.

1

2

3

4

5

6

2 Look and circle the words.

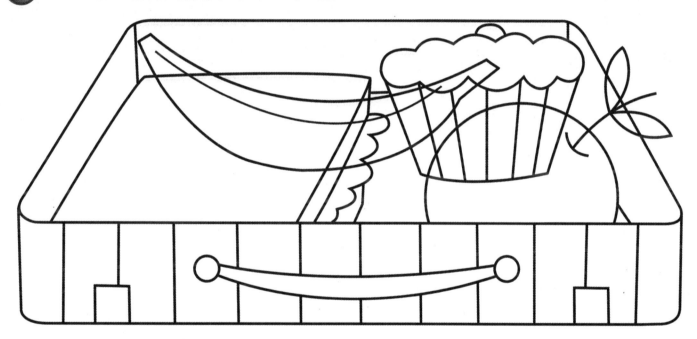

1 **I've got** / **haven't got** a sandwich.

2 **I've got** / **haven't got** a sausage.

3 **I've got** / **haven't got** an apple.

4 **I've got** / **haven't got** pizza.

5 **I've got** / **haven't got** a cake.

6 **I've got** / **haven't got** a banana.

1 **Number the pictures in the order of the song.**

2 **Look at the pictures and write the words.**

1 I've got _peas_
on my cake.

2 I've got _____
on my pizza.

3 I've got _____
in my milk.

4 I've got _____
in my cheese.

1 **Look at the picture and answer the questions.**

1 Have we got any cheese? — *Yes, we have.*

2 Have we got any apples? — *No, we haven't.*

3 Have we got any pizzas?

4 Have we got any milk?

5 Have we got any orange juice?

6 Have we got any sausages?

7 Have we got any steaks?

8 Have we got any bananas?

1 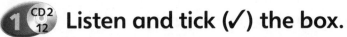 **Listen and tick (✓) the box.**

1

2

3

2 **Match the pictures with the sentences.**

a

b  3

c 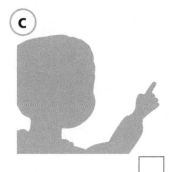 ☐

d  ☐

1 Thank you.

2 OK. Sausages and peas, please.

3 Mmm. Pizza. My favourite!

4 Pizza, please.

3 **Think!** **Write the numbers.**

1 I've got a cake.   ☐ Here you are.   ☐ Fantastic!

What have you got?

1

2

Chicken and carrots, please.

3

1 (Values) Look and circle.

2 CD2 14 Say and colour. Listen, point and say.

a = black   o = orange   e = red   i = pink

1 **Look at the numbers. Look at the letters. Write the words.**

① **13**   _thirteen_   e h t r i t n e

② **17**   _____   v e e n e e s n t

③ **15**   _____   t i n f e f e

④ **11**   _____   l e n v e e

⑤ **20**   _____   w e y t n t

⑥ **18**   _____   h i g e t e n e

1 Look at the menu and choose food you like.

I don't like sausage sandwiches.   I like chicken pizza.

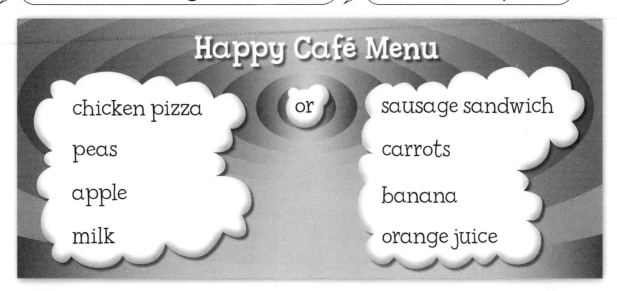

Happy Café Menu

chicken pizza   or   sausage sandwich

peas   carrots

apple   banana

milk   orange juice

2 Think! Match the sentences with the pictures. Write numbers.

1 I like pizza and peas. I don't like apples or milk.

2 I like pizza and carrots. I don't like bananas or milk.

3 I like sausages and carrots. I don't like bananas or orange juice.

4 I like sausages and peas. I don't like apples or milk.

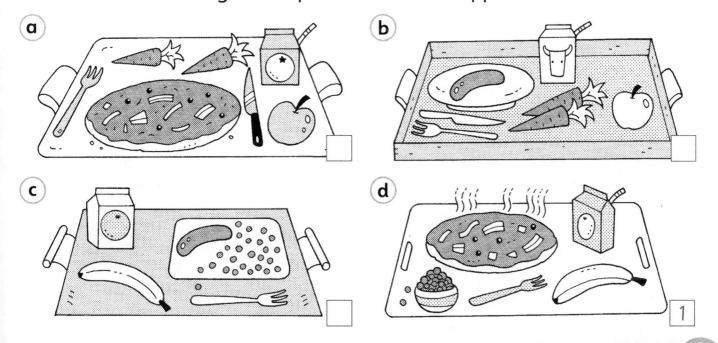

a

b

c

d 1

1 **Find the fruit and vegetables. Look → and ↓.**

corn

```
o  t  o  m  a  t  o  s  d  b
n  b  c  o  r  n  f  y  k  a
i  n  a  p  o  t  a  t  o  n
o  m  p  p  r  e  y  g  t  a
n  c  p  e  r  j  o  w  l  n
q  a  l  p  e  a  r  v  b  a
g  r  e  r  p  e  a  c  h  w
e  r  a  e  v  y  n  j  m  t
z  o  p  e  a  s  g  n  e  x
s  t  r  a  w  b  e  r  r  y
```

1 (Think!) **Colour the fruit red. Colour the vegetables green.**

○ peppers   ○ apples   ○ oranges   ○ carrots

○ onions   ○ strawberries   ○ peaches   ○ peas

○ tomatoes   ○ potatoes   ○ bananas   ○ pears

2 **Draw the fruit and vegetables on the trees, in the ground or on the plants.**

~~carrot~~   pepper   onion   pear   apple   potato   tomato

1 **Make a 3-D apple.**

You need

card   scissors   coloured pens   coloured paper   glue

1

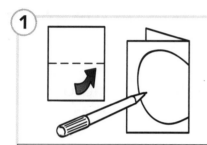

Fold the card in half. Draw half an apple.

2

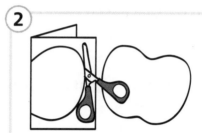

Cut out the apple. Cut out one more apple.

3

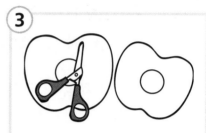

Cut a hole in the middle of each piece.

4

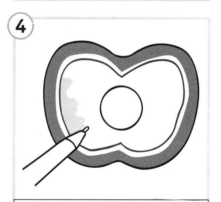

Colour the pieces.

5

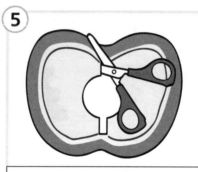

On one piece, cut from the core.

6

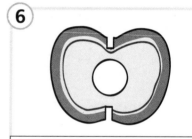

On the other piece, cut from the top and bottom.

7

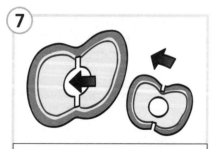

Put one piece into the core of the other piece.

8

Make seeds and leaves and stick on.

9

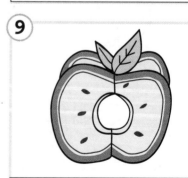

Now you have a 3-D apple.

My Super Mind

1 **Draw and write examples of what you know.**

1

I've got a cake and an apple.

2

3

4

5 Free time

1 Write the days of the week.

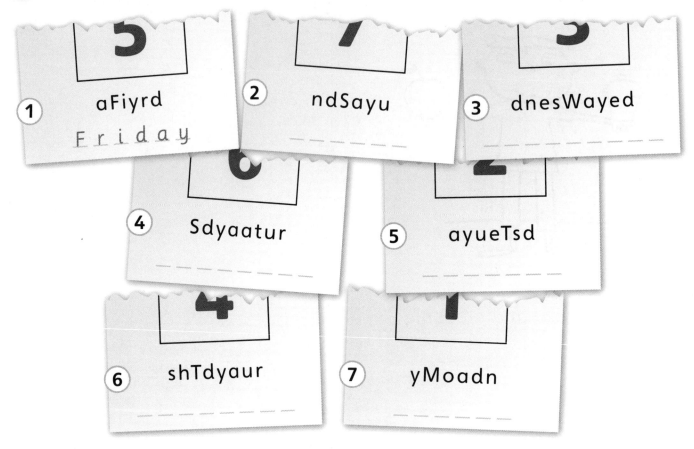

1. **aFiyrd**
   F r i d a y

2. **ndSayu**
   _____

3. **dnesWayed**
   _____

4. **Sdyaatur**
   _____

5. **ayueTsd**
   _____

6. **shTdyaur**
   _____

7. **yMoadn**
   _____

2 Draw your favourite day and write.

Friday

My favourite day is Friday.

_____

_____

Listen and tick (✓) the box.

1 Sue

2 Bob

3 Kate

4 Tim

Put the words in order.

1 Saturdays I on go swimming — *I go swimming on Saturdays.*

2 Fridays I play football on

3 I Sundays piano on play the

4 ride Tuesdays pony my on I

5 on I my Wednesdays ride bike

Free time activities 59

1 **Read the song and tick (✓) the box.**

1 On Mondays we

2 On Wednesdays we

3 On Fridays we

4 On Sundays we

2 **Write a new verse about you.**
Draw a picture.

On Mondays I _____ .

On Tuesdays I _____ .

On Wednesdays and on Thursdays,

I _____ .

1 **Write the words and tick (✓) the box.**

	Yes, I do.	No, I don't.

1 Do you _go_ swimming at the weekend? ☐ ☐

2 Do you _____ your bike at the weekend? ☐ ☐

3 Do you _____ football at the weekend? ☐ ☐

4 Do you _____ the piano at the weekend? ☐ ☐

5 Do you _____ with your toys at the weekend? ☐ ☐

6 Do you _____ TV at the weekend? ☐ ☐

2 **Follow the lines and find the answers to the questions.**

1 Do you play football at the weekend? _Yes_

2 Do you ride your bike at the weekend? _____

3 Do you play computer games at the weekend? _____

4 Do you ride a pony at the weekend? _____

5 Do you play in the park at the weekend? _____

6 Do you play ball at the weekend? _____

1 ^{CD2 28} **Listen and tick (✓) the box.**

1

2

3

2 **Circle the words.**

1 Where's the (lake) / frog?

2 Wait and swim / see.

3 Come with **Thunder / me**.

4 Are you OK, **rabbit / Misty?**

3 Think! **Write the sentences.**

I don't know.   Come with me.   Yes, I am.

1 Where's my bag?
I don't know.

2 Are you OK?
_____

3 Where's my classroom?
_____

1 (**Values**) **Look and circle.**

1

2

2 CD2 30 **Write the words. Listen and say.**

rat ~~duck~~ milk pens rubber hot dog

1 Mum and her
duck .

2 Ken and his
_____ .

3 Jill and her
_____ .

4 Polly and her
_____ .

5 Sam and his
_____ .

6 Thunder and his
_____ .

1 Draw lines.

1 On Mondays I play with   computer games.

2 On Tuesdays I ride   pony.

3 On Wednesdays I play   piano.

4 On Thursdays I go   friends.

5 On Fridays I ride my   TV.

6 On Saturdays I play the   swimming.

7 On Sundays I watch   my bike.

2 Look at Activity 1. Write the days.

a   b   c   d

Tuesday

e   f   g

1 **Listen and tick (✓) the box.**

1 On Mondays James

2 On Tuesdays Emma

3 On Wednesdays David

4 On Thursdays Amy

5 On Fridays Charles

6 On Saturdays and Sundays Hannah

1 Write *h* (healthy) or *u* (unhealthy).

1

h

2

_____

3

_____

4

_____

5

_____

6

_____

7

_____

8

_____

1 Think! Read and write the numbers.

My Week

On Mondays I watch TV for two hours. I play football for one hour and I read for one hour.

On Tuesdays I watch TV for three hours. I don't do sport and I read for two hours.

On Wednesdays I watch TV for one hour. I play tennis for one hour and I read for one hour.

On Thursdays I don't watch TV. I swim for one hour and I read for two hours.

On Fridays I watch TV for two hours. I play football for one hour, but I don't read.

On Saturdays and Sundays I do nothing!

1 I do sport for _four_ hours a week.

2 I watch TV for _____ hours a week.

3 I read for _____ hours a week.

Crafts

1 **Make a guitar.**

You need

tissue box

paint and brushes

elastic bands of different sizes

1

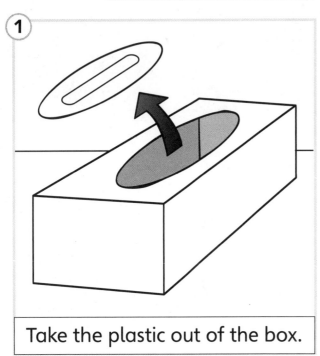

Take the plastic out of the box.

2

Paint the box.

3

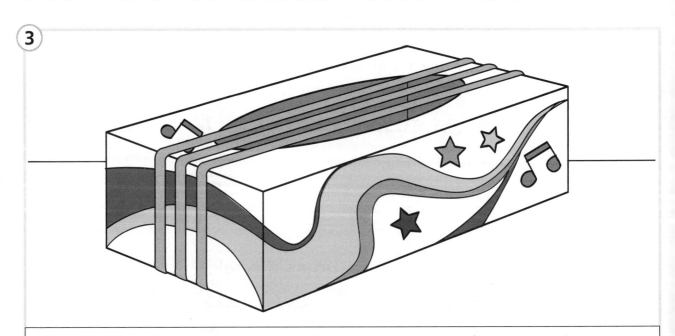

Put the elastic bands around the box. Now you have a guitar.

My Super Mind

1 Draw and write examples of what you know.

1

I ride my bike on Sundays.

2

3

4

6 The old house

1 **Write the words.**

bathroom   cellar   stairs   kitchen
living room   ~~hall~~   bedroom   dining room

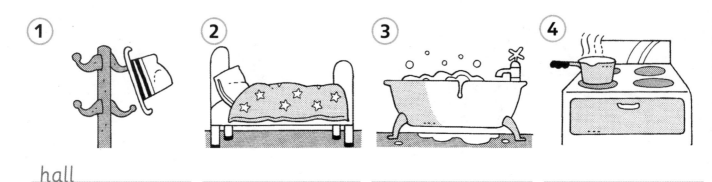

① hall _____

② _____

③ _____

④ _____

⑤ _____

⑥ _____

⑦ _____

⑧ _____

2 **Choose a room. Write and draw.**

Me in my living room

_____

1 **Listen and circle.**

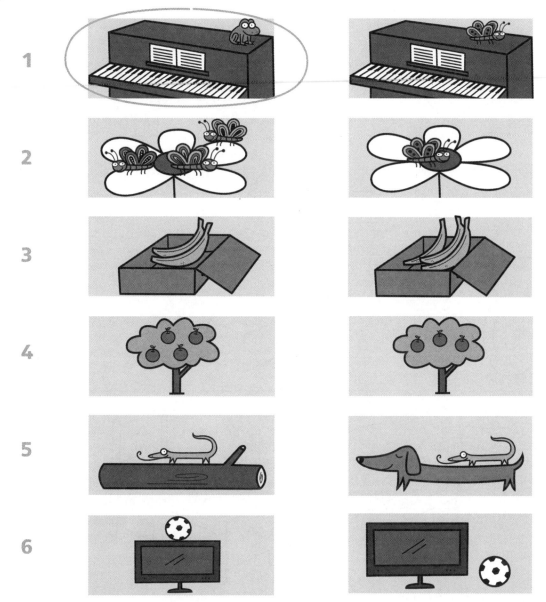

2 **Look at the pictures in Activity 1. Circle the words.**

1 (**There's**) / **There are** a frog on the piano.

2 **There's** / **There are** three butterflies on the flower.

3 **There's** / **There are** three bananas in the lunchbox.

4 **There's** / **There are** three apples on the tree.

5 **There's** / **There are** a lizard on the log.

6 **There's** / **There are** a football on the TV.

1 Read the song. Draw the animals.

1 **Look and tick (✓) the box.**

1 Is there a butterfly on a flower?

✓ Yes, there is.   ☐ No, there isn't.

2 Is there a frog on the log?

☐ Yes, there is.   ☐ No, there isn't.

3 Are there any bikes on the grass?

☐ Yes, there are.   ☐ No, there aren't.

4 Are there any bananas on the tree?

☐ Yes, there are.   ☐ No, there aren't.

2 **Look at the picture in Activity 1. Match the questions with the answers.**

1 Is there a spider on the flower?   **a** No, there aren't.

2 Are there any snakes in the garden? **b** No, there isn't.

3 How many apples are there?   **c** There are two.

4 How many bikes are there?   **d** There are eight.

1 **CD2 46** **Listen and tick (✓) the box.**

1

2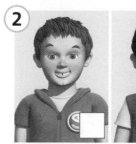

3

2 **Look and write the numbers.**

1 The stairs to the cellar! How many are there?

Eight.

2 Big spiders! How many are there?

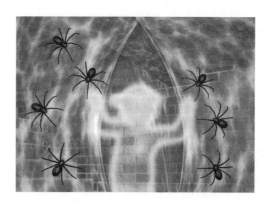

3 Big rats! How many are there?

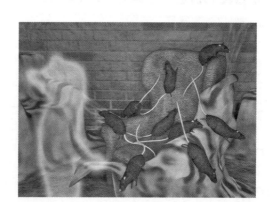

1 (Values) Look and circle.

1

2

2 CD2 48 **Write the words. Listen and say.**

house   hat   hot   happy   ~~hall~~   healthy

1 Harry's _hall_

2 A small _____

3 _____ food

4 A _____ frog

5 A _____ pizza

6 An old _____

1 **Listen and colour.**

1 **Look and read. Write *yes* or *no*.**

1 There are two boys and two girls.   yes

2 The children have got ice creams.   no

3 The boys have got a ball.

4 The girls have got bikes.

5 There is a cat in the tree.

6 There are three dogs in the park.

7 There are three butterflies on the flower.

1 **Write the letters.**

1 jungle **2** d_s_rt **3** m_unt_ins

4 p_lar regi_n **5** _ce_n

2 **Match the words with the pictures.**

a

1 sand

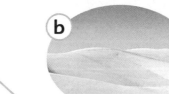

b

2 coral

3 snow

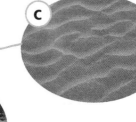

c

4 rocks

d

5 trees

e

1 **Write the words.**

goat polar bear ~~tiger~~ parrot
shark camel jellyfish penguin

1 tiger

2 _____

3 _____

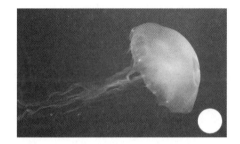

4 _____

5 _____

6 _____

7 _____

8 _____

2 **Think!** **Colour the circles in Activity 1.**

Key

grey = polar regions   blue = oceans   yellow = deserts

red = mountains   green = jungle

1 **Make a pop-up house.**

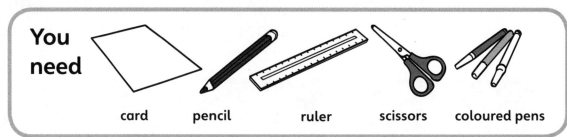

You need

card   pencil   ruler   scissors   coloured pens

1

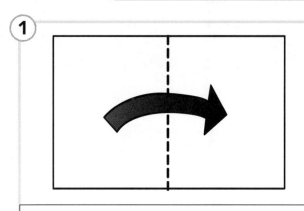

Fold the card in half.

2

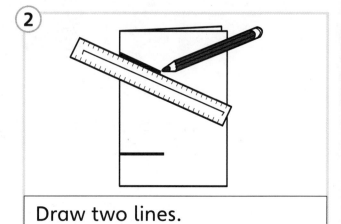

Draw two lines.

3

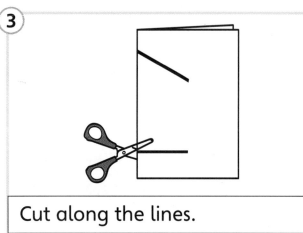

Cut along the lines.

4

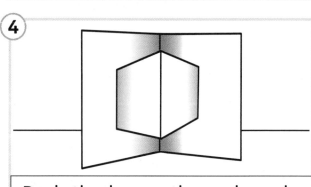

Push the house through and fold.

5

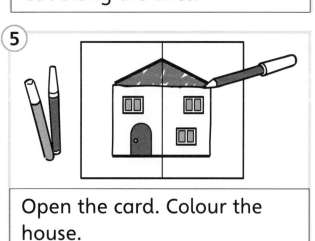

Open the card. Colour the house.

6

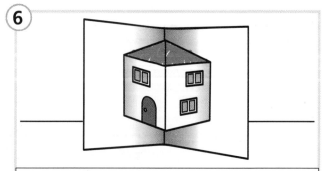

Now you have a pop-up house.

My Super Mind

1 **Draw and write examples of what you know.**

1

There's a jellyfish in the ocean.

2

3

4

7 Get dressed!

1 Find the clothes. Look → and ↓.

T-shirt _____ _____ _____

h	u	s	o	c	k	s	j	h
T	s	h	i	r	t	k	a	f
w	j	e	a	n	s	i	c	x
r	i	w	v	e	b	r	k	s
l	c	a	p	n	z	t	e	h
m	s	h	o	r	t	s	t	o
q	s	w	e	a	t	e	r	e
y	t	r	o	u	s	e	r	s

 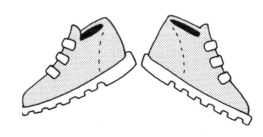 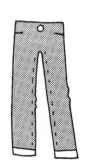

_____ _____ _____

1 Match the pictures with the sentences. Write numbers.

① ② ③ ④

☐ I like these T-shirts.	☐ 1 I like this T-shirt.
☐ I don't like this T-shirt.	☐ I don't like these T-shirts.

2 Circle the words.

1 Do you like **this** / **these** cap?

2 Do you like **this** / **these** jeans?

3 Do you like **this** / **these** shoes?

4 Do you like **this** / **these** skirt?

5 Do you like **this** / **these** jacket?

6 Do you like **this** / **these** socks?

1 **Read, dress and colour.**

Polly

Molly

| **Polly** | red hat | blue sweater | pink skirt | yellow socks | red shoes |
| **Molly** | blue cap | black jacket | orange jeans | yellow T-shirt | green shoes |

1 **Read and write the names.**

1 _____ 2 _____ 3 _Amy_____ 4 _____

Amy is wearing a shirt and a sweater. She is wearing a skirt, socks and shoes.

Terry is wearing a cap, a shirt and a sweater. She is wearing jeans, socks and shoes.

Clare is wearing a T-shirt and a jacket. She is wearing a skirt, socks and shoes.

Naomi is wearing a shirt and a sweater. She is wearing jeans, socks and shoes.

2 **Look at the pictures in Activity 1. Tick (✓) the box.**

1 Is Amy wearing a jacket?

☐ Yes, she is.   ✓ No, she isn't.

2 Is Clare wearing a skirt?

☐ Yes, she is.   ☐ No, she isn't.

3 Is Terry wearing jeans?

☐ Yes, she is.   ☐ No, she isn't.

4 Are Naomi and Amy wearing caps?

☐ Yes, they are.   ☐ No, they aren't.

1 ^{CD3 11} **Listen and tick (✓) the box.**

1

2

3

2 (Think!) **Write the names. Who is wearing … ?**

1 these shoes?   **2** this cap?   **3** this skirt?

  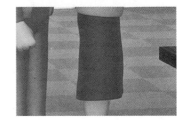

_____ _____ _____

3 **Match the dialogues with the pictures.**

1 **A:** That's my book.
B: I'm sorry.

2 **A:** My shoes aren't here.
B: Oh no!

3 **A:** Get my bag, please.
B: No problem.

4 **A:** Sheila's wearing my jacket.
B: Are you sure?

a

b

c

d

1

1 ⬤ Values ⬠ Look and circle.

I'm sorry.

2 CD 3 13 **Write the letters. Listen and say.**

st sw sk st sp sch st sn

1 st op

2 ___ider

3 ___eak

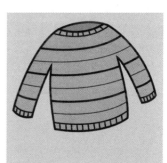

4 ___eater

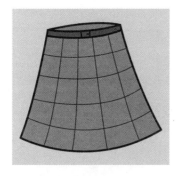

5 ___irt

6 ___airs

7 ___ool

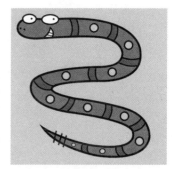

8 ___ake

1   **Read the poem and colour the picture.**

This red T-shirt,

These blue trousers,

These black shoes

And these blue socks.

Let's put them all

In this box.

2   **Think!**   **Write your poem and draw a picture.**

This _____ _____ ,

These _____ _____ ,

These _____ _____

And these _____ _____ .

Let's put them all

In this box.

1 Look at the pictures and read the questions.
Write one-word answers.

1 What's the boy doing?

   He is _eating_ .

2 Where are the boy and the girl?

   In the _____ .

3 What is the boy doing?

   He is playing computer

   _____ .

4 What's the girl doing?

   She is watching _____ .

5 How many cats are there?

   There are _____ .

6 Where are the cats?

   Under the _____ .

1 **Write the word *cotton*, *wool* or *leather*.**

1

2

3

cotton

4

5

6

2 **Read. Then write and draw.**

I'm wearing a cotton T-shirt, cotton jeans, woollen socks and leather shoes.

1 **Find out about your clothes. Complete the chart.**

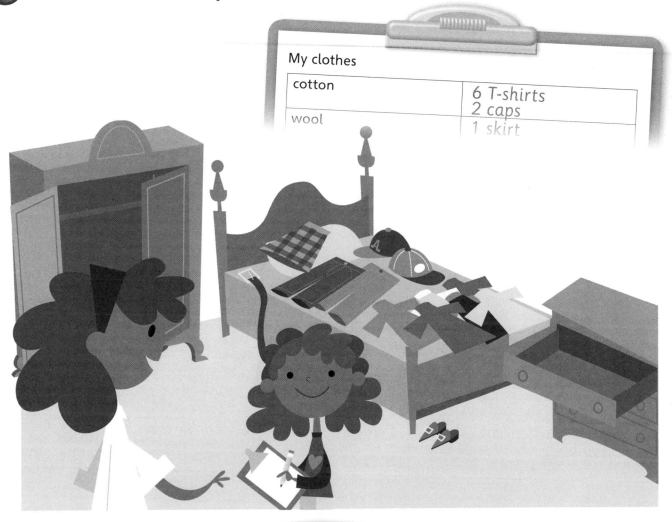

My clothes

cotton	6 T-shirts 2 caps
wool	1 skirt

My clothes

cotton	
wool	
leather	

Crafts

1 **Make a paper hat.**

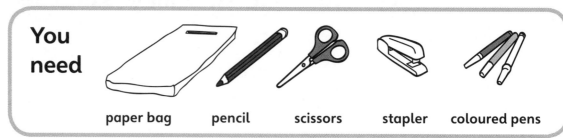

You need   paper bag   pencil   scissors   stapler   coloured pens

1

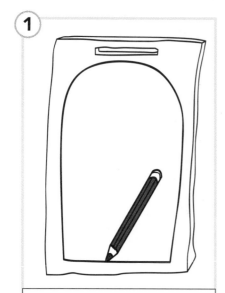

Draw a hat on the bag.

2

Cut out the two pieces.

3

Your teacher staples the hat.

4

Colour the hat.

5

Now you have a paper hat.

My Super Mind

1 Draw and write examples of what you know.

1

Do you like this sweater?

Yes, I do.

2

3

4

1 Write the letters to make parts of the body.

h	e	a	d			o	o	
	a				i			o
k		e	e		n			e
	d			l	e			s
					e			
			a		m			

t n f g r h

2 Write the words.

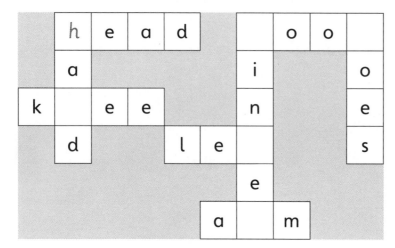

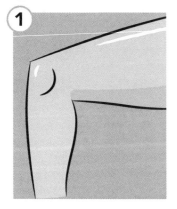 1
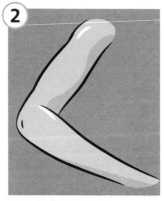 2
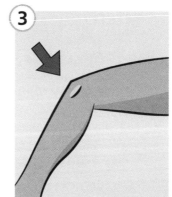 3
 4

leg _____

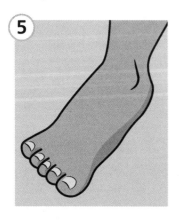 5
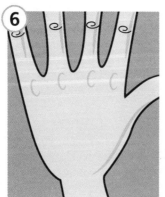 6
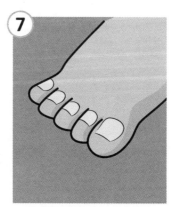 7
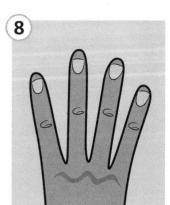 8

_____ _____ _____ _____

1 Write the numbers.

1 I can stand on one leg.

2 I can skip.

3 I can touch my toes.

4 I can't stand on one leg.

5 I can't skip.

6 I can't touch my toes.

1 **Match the pictures with the sentences. Colour the circles.**

◯ I can dance.   ◯ I can crawl.   ◯ I can run.

◯ I can swim.   ◯ I can jump up high.   ⬤ I can sing.

1 **Complete the questions.**

1 <u>Can</u> he play the piano?

☐ Yes, he can. ✓ No, he can't.

2 _____ dance?

☐ Yes, she can. ☐ No, she can't.

3 _____ swim?

☐ Yes, he can. ☐ No, he can't.

4 _____ a horse?

☐ Yes, she can. ☐ No, she can't.

5 _____ tennis?

☐ Yes, he can. ☐ No, he can't.

6 _____ ?

☐ Yes, she can. ☐ No, she can't.

2 **Look at the pictures in Activity 1. Answer the questions.**

1 🎧 CD3 27 Listen and tick (✓) the box.

1

2

3

2 Write the words.

you   done   ~~right~~   problem

Here's the _right_ leg.

1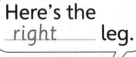

No _____ .

2

Here _____ are.

3

Well _____ , Misty.

4

3 Write the numbers.

☐ What are you doing?   ☐ I've got a problem.

1 Let's go for a horse ride.   ☐ No problem.

1
Great idea.

2
Let me try something.

3
Wait and see.

Thanks.

4

Values Look and circle.

2 ^{CD3} 29 **Write and match. Listen and say.**

a

b

1 _g_ rey

2 fro___

3 computer ___ame

4 ___arden

5 fin___ers

6 le___

7 do___

e

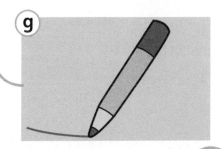
f

c

d

g

1 (Think!) **Read and tick (✓) or cross (✗).**

Hi, I'm Jerry. I can touch my toes, but I can't skip. I can play tennis and football, but I can't play the piano. I can ride a bike, but I can't ride a horse.

Hi, I'm Stacey. I can skip, but I can't touch my toes. I can play the piano and I can play tennis, but I can't play football. I can ride a bike and I can ride a horse.

Hi, I'm Tom. I can touch my toes and I can skip. I can play tennis and I can play football, but I can't play the piano. I can ride a bike, but I can't ride a horse.

	touch toes	skip	play the piano	play football	play tennis	ride a bike	ride a horse
Jerry	✓						
Stacey							
Tom							

2 **Look at Activity 1. Tick (✓) the box.**

1 Jerry, can you skip? ☐ Yes, I can. ✓ No, I can't.

2 Jerry, can you ride a bike? ☐ Yes, I can. ☐ No, I can't.

3 Stacey, can you touch your toes? ☐ Yes, I can. ☐ No, I can't.

4 Stacey, can you play tennis? ☐ Yes, I can. ☐ No, I can't.

5 Tom, can you ride a horse? ☐ Yes, I can. ☐ No, I can't.

6 Tom, can you play the piano? ☐ Yes, I can. ☐ No, I can't.

1 **Read the questions. Listen and write a name or a number.**

1 What's the girl's name?   *Karen*

2 How old is she?

3 What's the dog's name?

4 How many lizards has the girl got?

5 What's the horse's name?

1 **Write the words.**

jumping dancing sitting swimming
~~playing the piano~~ riding a bike

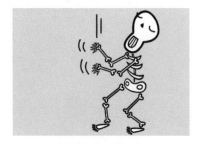

1 It's *playing the piano.*

2 It's _____

3 It's _____

4 It's _____

_____

5 It's _____

6 It's _____

2 **Match the words with the pictures.**

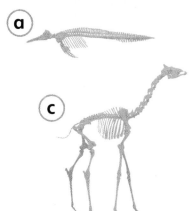

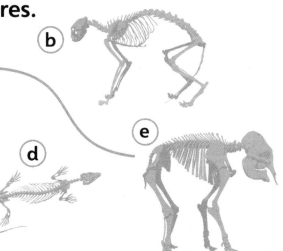

1 elephant

2 giraffe

3 dolphin

4 tiger

5 lizard

1 **Think!** **Write the numbers.**

1 leg

2 arm

3 knee

4 head

5 foot

6 hand

7 toe

8 finger

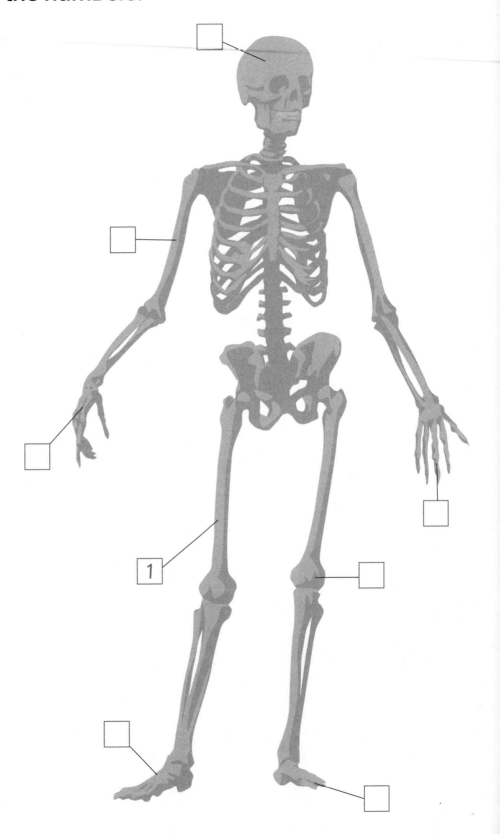

1 **Make a robot mask.**

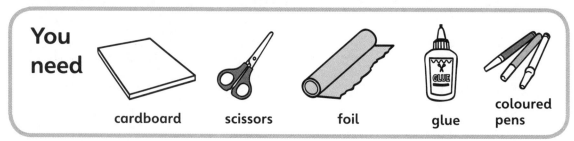

You need

cardboard   scissors   foil   glue   coloured pens

1

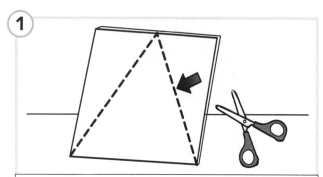

Cut a triangle out of the cardboard.

2

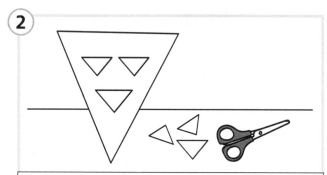

Your teacher cuts out eyes and a mouth.

3

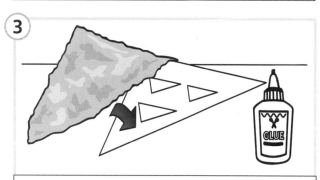

Stick the foil onto the cardboard.

4

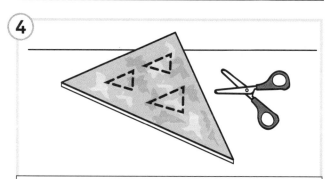

Cut the foil to make the eyes and mouth.

5

Colour the mask.

6

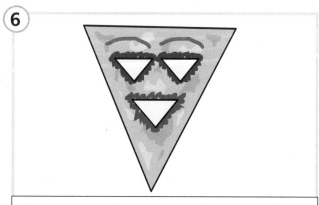

Now you have a robot mask.

My Super Mind

1 **Draw and write examples of what you know.**

1

I can dance.

2

3

4

9 At the beach

1 **Write the words.**

①
look for _shells_

②
take a _____

③
catch a _____

④
paint a _____

⑤
listen to _____

⑥
eat _____

⑦
read a _____

⑧
make a _____

2 **Read. Then write and draw.**

I'm eating ice cream.

_____

1 Complete the sentences with the words.

make ~~read~~ read make catch

1 **A:** Let's _read_ a book.
   B: Good idea.

2 **A:** Let's _____ a book.
   B: Sorry, I don't want to.

3 **A:** Let's _____ a sandcastle.
   B: Good idea.

4 **A:** Let's _____ a sandcastle.
   B: Sorry, I don't want to.

5 **A:** Let's _____ a fish.
   B: I'm not sure.

2 Match the pictures with the dialogues in Activity 1. Number the pictures.

4

1 Write more lines for the song. Draw pictures.

1 Let's *play the guitar* .

2 Let's _____ .

3 Let's _____ .

4 Let's _____ .

5 Let's _____ .

6 Let's _____ .

1 **Think!** Look at the pictures and match the questions with the answers.

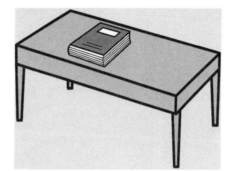

1 Where's the guitar?

2 Where are the shells?

3 Where's the fish?

4 Where are the birds?

5 Where's the book?

6 Where's the shell?

7 Where's the photo?

8 Where's the ice cream?

a It's in the book.

b It's in the sea.

c They're on the sandcastle.

d It's on his T-shirt.

e It's on the bed.

f It's on the sandcastle.

g It's on the desk.

h They're in the box.

1  **Listen and tick (✓) the box.**

1     **2**     **3**

2 **Write the words.**

> Bye. See you at the _top_ of the hill!

> This is the end of the _____ .

> Now you can race to the top, _____ !

> What a _____ idea!

1    **2**    **3**    **4**

3 **Think!** **Write the numbers.**

☐ A race is not a good idea.   ☐ Let me try.   1 Wait and see.

> What's that?

> I can't do it.

> Let's race!

3

1

2

1 (Values) Look and circle.

2 CD3 8 46 **Write and match. Listen and say.**

a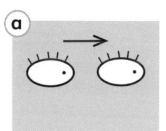

b

1 thr_ee_

2 b____ch

3 s____

4 p___s

5 r____d

6 ice cr____m

7 ___t

8 ch____se

f

g

h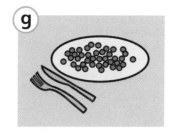

c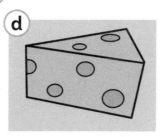

d

e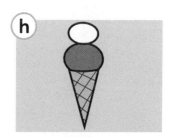

1 CD3 48 Listen and write the names.

Kay   Pip   Tom   Bob   ~~Jim~~   Sue   Liz   Mia

a _____

b _____

c _____

d _____

e _____

f Jim_____

g _____

h _____

1 **Read this. Choose a word from the box. Write the correct word next to numbers 1–5.**

It's a lovely day on the beach. The _sun_ is hot and the

(1)_____ is cool. There are lots of children on the beach. One

boy is making a (2)_____ . It's very big. There is a little girl.

She is wearing a (3)_____ on her head and she is eating an

(4)_____ . There is a man. He is playing a (5)_____ .

What a lovely day at the beach!

shell   sun   hat   sea

guitar   castle   sandcastle   ice cream

1 Think! Use the code to write the words.

◗ ● ☼ ☼ ✳
1 s u n n y

✪ 🌈 ♠
2 _ _ _

◆ 🌈 ♥ ◖
3 _ _ _ _

◗ ☼ 🌈 ✸ ▼ ☼ O
4 _ _ _ _ _ _ _

◆ ♥ 🌈 ● ◖ ✳
5 _ _ _ _ _ _

☁ / ▼ ☼ ▼ ☼ O
6 _ _ _ _ _ _ _

Code

a = /	h = ✪	o = 🌈	u = ●
c = ◆	i = ▼	r = ☁	w = ✸
d = ◖	l = ♥	s = ◗	y = ✳
g = O	n = ☼	t = ♠	

2 Write the words.

1 cloudy

2 _____

3 _____

4 _____

5 _____

6 _____

1 Read and draw the symbols on the map.

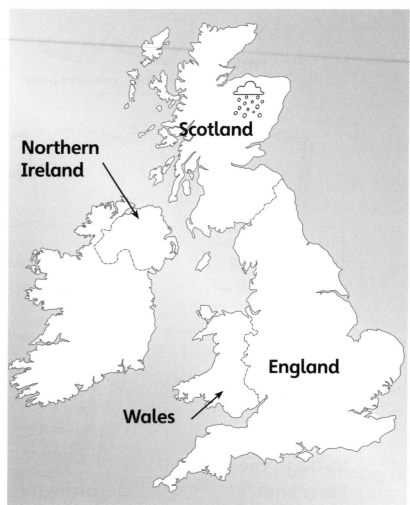

1 It's snowing in Scotland and it's cold.

2 It's cold and cloudy in Wales.

3 It's raining and cloudy in England.

4 It's hot and sunny in Northern Ireland.

2 Read. Then write a postcard to your friend.

Dear Tom
How are you?
It's cloudy
and cold
today.
Bye,
Sam

40

40

Crafts

1 **Make a holiday scrapbook.**

You need white paper  coloured paper hole punch string coloured pens photos

1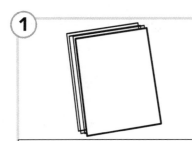
Put the white paper together.

2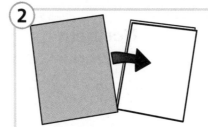
Put the coloured paper on top.

3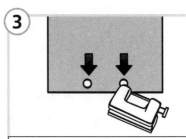
Make two holes in the paper.

4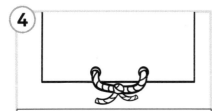
Put the string through the holes. Tie a knot.

5
Decorate the cover.

6
Now you have a holiday scrapbook.

2 **Draw pictures or stick in photographs. Write sentences.**

Monday
The beach
I love the beach! It's sunny. I eat ice cream and swim in the sea.

Tuesday
The garden
I like my garden. I read and play ball.

My Super Mind

1 Draw and write examples of what you know.

1

Goodbye ice cream!

2

3

4

Friends

nine   two   ~~one~~   seven   four   five   three   eight   ten   six

1

one

2

3

4

5

6

7

8

9

10

At school

notebook ~~bag~~ ruler desk book
pencil case pencil rubber pen

bag

Let's play!

car doll kite ~~ball~~ computer game
plane go-kart bike monster train

ball _____ _____

_____ _____ _____ _____

_____ _____ _____

Pet show

rat   duck   frog   lizard   ~~cat~~   elephant   spider   dog

cat _____   _____   _____

_____   _____   _____

_____   _____

Lunchtime

chicken   peas   carrots   pizza   cheese sandwich
~~apples~~   sausages   cake   steak   bananas

apples _____   _____

_____   _____   _____   _____

_____   _____   _____

nineteen ~~eleven~~ twelve eighteen fourteen
fifteen thirteen seventeen twenty sixteen

11 12 13

eleven

14 15 16 17

18 19 20

5 Free time

Monday ~~Monday~~ Friday Sunday Tuesday
Wednesday Saturday Thursday

Monday

Tuesday

Wednesday

Thursday

Monday

Friday

Saturday

Sunday

The old house

dining room   living room   cellar   bedroom
kitchen   ~~bathroom~~   hall   stairs

bathroom

Get dressed!

shorts   socks   jeans   ~~cap~~   trousers
skirt   T-shirt   shoes   jacket   sweater

cap

The robot

leg ~~arm~~ toes head fingers hand knee foot

 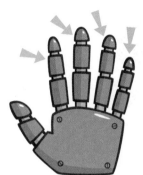  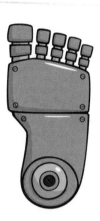

arm _____

_____ _____

  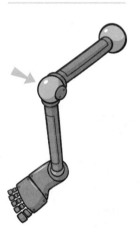

_____ _____ _____

 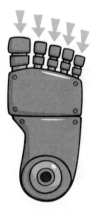

_____ _____

At the beach

paint a picture   ~~catch a fish~~   take a photo   listen to music
eat ice cream   read a book   look for shells   make a sandcastle

catch a fish